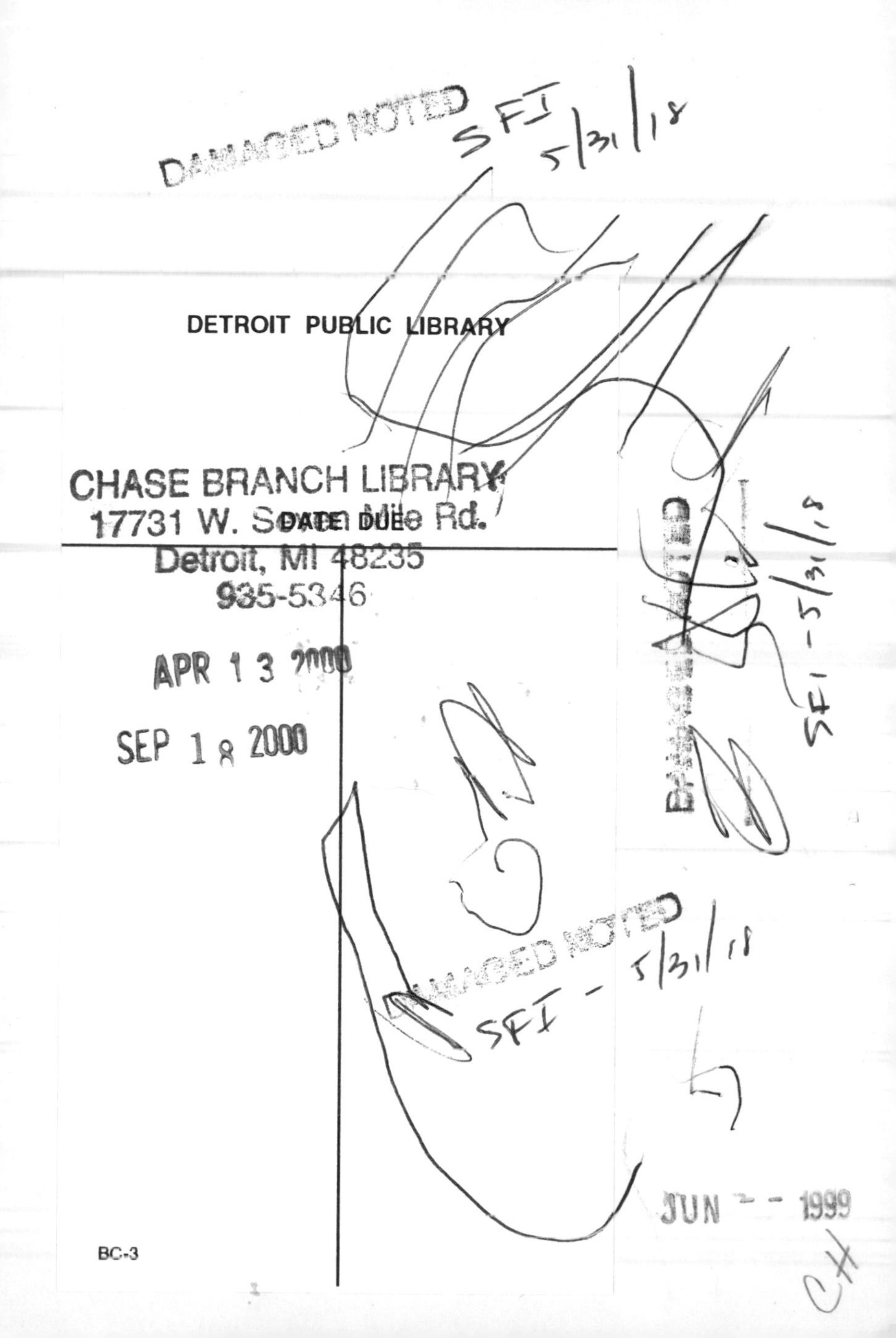
DAMAGED NOTED SFI 5/31/18
DETROIT PUBLIC LIBRARY
CHASE BRANCH LIBRARY
17731 W. Seven Mile Rd.
DATE DUE
Detroit, MI 48235
935-5346
APR 1 3 2000
SEP 1 8 2000
DAMAGED NOTED SFI - 5/31/18
JUN 2 - 1999
BC-3

Contents

1. JUST ASKING

Is the hot dog a gambler?
Yes, he believes in wiener takes all.

Why don't you exercise more?
I do. I lift my eyebrows, jump to conclusions, and raise cane.

Where are you going with that weighing machine?
I'm going to scale a mountain.

What is the weeping willow's favorite month?
Wept-ember.

What is a star's favorite month?
Nova-ember.

What is a prisoner's favorite month?
Free-cember.

Did you ever see a sidewalk?
No, but I've seen a nose run.

What did one clock say to another?
I'm all wound up.

My grandfather is living on borrowed time.
Can't he find an apartment?

What did one fireplace say to another?
Stop making an ash of yourself.

Why do people cry at airports?
They're saying goodbye to their luggage.

How does a mirror travel on an airplane?
First glass.

What kind of trouble occurred after the Garden of Eden?
Cain dis-Abel-ed his brother.

Can I have five dollars? I'm a little short today.
Will you be a little taller tomorrow?

What would you use if you wanted to hit someone in the stomach?
A tummy-hawk.

What's the favorite magazine for sailors?
Ports Illustrated.

Why is a spoon always in trouble?

It stirs things up.

Why does a doormat say hello and goodbye?

For people who don't know whether they're coming or going.

Why was the broom late for work?

It overswept.

Where do insects drive their cars in California?

On the flea way.

How does an undertaker greet his customers?

Good mourning!

Do you ever go ice fishing?

No, I never need any ice.

How can you leave the house with two legs and come back with six?

Return with a chair.

What room in a house is used for complaints?

The whining room.

Why did the lawyer take his watch apart?

He wanted to rest his case.

What did one slice of bread say to another?

Don't look now, but a piece of ham is coming between us.

How do you like the lobster?

Less expensive.

How did you get run over?

My brother wouldn't go to the store for me, so I ran over myself.

What's the farmer's main concern at tax time?

Capital grains.

Why is the bald eagle thankful?

He has no dandruff.

How does the Devil greet people?

Hell-o!

How does a boxer travel in a plane?

Fist class.

What did the parrot say when it broke into the computer?

Polly want a hacker.

Is your watch going steady?
No, it has another date.

How did your watch stop?
It came to a red light.

Why did you get a blank piece of paper in the mail from Joe?
He's still not talking to me.

If a man wears pajamas, what does a woman wear?
Majamas.

How badly were you hurt?
I don't know. I haven't seen my lawyer yet.

What kind of wedding did the telephones have?
A double-ring ceremony.

Why didn't the pacifist light the fire?
He didn't want to strike a match.

What kind of job does a construction worker have?
He takes his pick.

How does a bee part his hair?
With a honeycomb.

What do you do with your plants while you're on vacation?
I have my parrot talk to them.

How did the man who was shot from a cannon die?
He was fired.

What job did the card player get on the cruise ship?
Deck hand.

Are you a racist?

No, I walk very slowly.

What did Rip Van Winkle say to his wife when she woke him up after he slept for 100 years?

Just five more minutes, dear.

I'm a coin collector. Are you?

Yes. Let's get together and talk over old dimes.

What is the chicken's favorite riddle?

Why did the man cross the road?

Why do you want to borrow sweet corn?

So I can lend an ear.

When will the mail arrive?

Sooner or letter.

What kind of music do policemen prefer?
Cop-era.

What did one antique dealer say to another?
Hello, Sam. What's old?

Why does history keep repeating itself?
Because it has a speech defect.

Is the hot dog outspoken?
Yes, he's very frank.

What's a gunman's favorite math subject?
Trigger-nometry.

Where do trombone players in an orchestra sit?
Slide by slide.

Are the fish biting?
No, they had their teeth out.

Are finance companies successful?
Yes. You have to give them a lot of credit.

What happened at Custer's Last Stand?
He had a markdown sale.

What are you going to be when you grow up?
A taxpayer.

May I have a pita bread?
Yes, but cut out the baby talk.

What does a tired Santa say?
Ho. Ho.

How do you make a windowbox?

Get him a trainer.

How do you get to the cemetery?

You die.

Have you noticed how much purer country air is?

Yes, it's a wonder they didn't build the city out there.

2. WHINING AND DINING

The food is so crummy and you sell it so cheap. Where do you make a profit?
We sell bicarbonate of soda.

Waiter, what's that fly doing in my soup?
He had a reservation.

Waiter, why is that fly drowning in my soup?
I'll get a lifeguard.

Waiter, what's that fly doing in my soup?
Skinny dipping.

Waiter, did you know this steak is half raw?
So eat the half that's cooked.

Waiter, what's that fly doing in my soup?
Don't worry, the hot water will kill it.

How does the Irish waiter greet you?
Tip of the morning to you!

Waiter, why is there a dime in my soup?
Would you rather have two nickels?

Would you make my corned beef lean?
Which way, sir, left or right?

Waiter, why are these peas cold?
I'll be right back with a pea jacket.

Did you like the frogs' legs?
Yes, but it was hard getting the shoes off.

Why do you always order asparagus in a restaurant?
I always leave a tip.

Don't you want your soup?
No, I heard the cook say he had a hand in making it.

Waiter, is this tea or coffee?
What does it taste like?
It tastes like turpentine.
That's coffee. The tea tastes like brake fluid.

Waiter, do you know it's been 10 years since I came here?
It's not my fault. I'm working as fast as I can.

What did your Chinese fortune cookie say?
Made in Japan.

What is England's favorite dessert?
Ice cream scone.

Have you finished your soup?
Yes, and give my compliments to the dishwasher.

What is Florida's favorite drink?
Pensa-Cola.

What's your favorite seafood?
Saltwater taffy.

What do you call an eating place for birds?
A nest-aurant.

Do you drink your coffee with milk?
No, I drink it alone.

What's the waiter doing in jail?
Serving time.

Waiter, did you know this coffee is very weak?
It's been sick.

Waiter, why is your hand in my soup?
I'm looking for dead flies.

Waiter, will you get this fly out of my soup?
You'll have to ask him yourself, we're not speaking.

Why did the restaurant hire midget waitresses?
To make the sandwiches look bigger.

Waiter, can I see the manager?
Sorry, but he's home recovering from food poisoning.

Waiter, what's taking so long for my sunny-side-up eggs?
It's a little cloudy out.

Waiter, do you know there's a fly in my soup?
That's OK, so long as he's not over his head.

Waiter, I found a fly in the soup. What are you going to do about it?
If no one claims it, it's yours.

Waiter, can you do something about this fly in my soup?
I'll call the bouncer.

Waiter, what's the difference between the $15 steak and the $30 one?

The $30 one has meat on it.

What's shaky and green, has 14 legs, and is covered with slime?

I don't know, but we're having it for lunch.

May I have a bite of your muffin?

Muffin doing.

3. ANIMAL CRACKERS

How did the snake decorate his bathroom?
With crawlpaper.

Were there any ants in your house?
Only one, but it had a big funeral.

What did one clam say to another?
When are you going to come out of your shell?

What do you say to the dogcatcher when you leave him?
Have a nice stray.

Why was the duck fired?
He was always lying down on the job.

What is a chicken's favorite day?
Hens-day.

What is a bird's favorite musical comedy?
Nest Side Story.

Where does a smart skunk work?
In a stink tank.

Why are you returning the dog you bought?
The mailman keeps biting him.

What do you call a hog that's a thief?
A pigpocket.

What do you get if you cross a night bird with a leopard?
A spotted owl.

What part of a song do skunks like best?
The smell-ody.

What does a donkey minister say to his flock?
"Let us bray."

Is the skunk talkative?
No, he's a creature of phew words.

How does a pig take a bath?
Unwillingly.

Is there anything you want to know about the horse?
Saddle do for now.

What is a skunk's favorite children's book?
Winnie the Phew.

How did the fish die?
It was an act of Cod.

Why don't you sleep with your pet skunk?
He snores.

What key does a hornet sing in?
Bee sharp.

How do you stop a mule from kicking?
Take away his soccer ball.

Where did the rodent go?
He went rat-away.

What did one duck say to the other?

When do you start growing down?

What fish likes to kiss?

A smack-erel.

How do you know the wallet you found was the snake's?

He said it was hiss.

Did you hear about the duck that drowned in Australia?

He went down under.

Why did the leopard go to the dry cleaner?

To get the spot out.

What's the matter with the sheep?

Bleats me.

How soon did the horse fall asleep?
As soon as he hit the hay.

Is the duck running for re-election?
No, it's stepping down.

How do you put an elephant in a mailbox?
Put him in a stamped envelope.

Why was the elephant kicked off the basketball team?
He took up too much space on the bench.

Why did the elephant walk up 10 flights of stairs?
The elevator was out of order.

When does a pig watch television?
In slime time.

What do you call a big gray animal that's always hollering?
A yell-ephant.

Does the skunk like the pool?
No, he'd rather stink than swim.

What game do fish play at parties?
Fried and seek.

Why does a pig always have ink on him?
You would too if you slept in a pen.

How did the elephant get to the top of the tree?
He climbed on the squirrel's back.

Is the octopus ready to fight?
Yes, he's well armed.

What did the student say when the skunk enrolled at Princeton?

P. U.

What do you call a cat in love?

A smitten kitten.

What did the butterfly study in college?

Math-ematics.

Where does a Boston sheep go for his liquor?

To the baa.

What does a skunk think of his wife's looks?

Phew-tiful.

Why do elephants walk to school?

They can't fit in the bus.

What do you call a fish that knows everything?
A sharp carp.

What is a skunk's favorite weapon?
A stink bomb.

Are there many skunks around?
No, they are phew and far between.

What do you call a toad who becomes a fortune-teller?
A frog-nosticator.

Why did the elephant slide down the banister?
The stairs were being fixed.

What is a duck's favorite state?
Ken-duck-y.

How much did you pay for the deer?
One thousand bucks.

Does your dog have a good pedigree?
If he could talk, he wouldn't speak to any of us.

What does a rabbit do in the hot weather?
It puts on the hare conditioner.

Did the rabbit win the race by much?
By a hare.

What did one leopard say to another?
Don't look now but I think the cops have spotted us.

What position does the king of the jungle play in football?
Lion backer.

What did the bee say to its little sister?
Let me bee.

How is the zebra doing in the army?
He earned his stripes.

How did the goat make out in school?
Not too good. He was always kidding around.

What happened when you put your hand in the lion's mouth?
He told me to take it out and wash it.

Why is the duck so brave?
He might be down but he's never out.

What do you say to your cat when you leave your house?
Have a mice day.

What is a horse's favorite avenue?
Mane Street.

How does a cat clean his paint brush?
With purr-pentine.

What job does a bird get in construction?
Crane operator.

Who entertains at a mouse convention?
An after-dinner squeaker.

Has your dog got papers?
No, only magazines.

Has your dog any papers?
Yes, all over the floor.

What does the leopard do on TV?
On-the-spot news.

What's the dog doing out behind the house?
Shedding.

How did the hen do as a stand-up comic?
She laid an egg.

Why did the elephant take the mouse to the movies?
The dog couldn't go.

Why is the dog wearing glasses?
Because he couldn't read the eye chart.

Where does the skunk put his dirty dishes?
In the kitchen stink.

Did they find the hen who's a gangster?
No, she's laying low.

Why was the elephant refused a driver's license?
He couldn't buckle his seat belt.

What does a blackbird do every day?
Crows older.

How was the skunk who fainted revived?
With smelling salts.

How did the horse save up so much money?
Bit by bit.

What did one dog say to another?
Stop hounding me.

What does a snake use for a gun?
A hiss-tol.

What does a deer have in its mouth?
Buck teeth.

Why was the hen arrested?
She was an egg beater.

What is the skunk's favorite contest?
A smelling bee.

How does a cosmetic clerk eat Chinese food?
With Chap Sticks.

How does a lumberjack eat Chinese food?
With chopsticks.

What did the horse say to his jockey?
Get off my back.

Where does an Eskimo keep his hog?
In a pig-loo.

How does the leopard keep house?
Spotless.

4. LAUGH IT UP

What did one snowball say to another?
Stop acting flaky.

What happened on the Fourth of July?
I don't know. I was at camp.

Why is the car knocking?
We don't have a doorbell.

Why does your bed get longer at night?
Because two feet are added to it.

Why is the carpet on the ceiling?
So it won't wear out.

How come you stay after school so much?
I can't stay before school.

Why are you riding your bike in this heavy traffic?
I'm not allowed to cross the street alone.

What is a tailor's favorite breakfast cereal?
Coat-meal.

Did you notice the moon was down to its last quarter?
Yes, I think we should take up a collection for it.

What magazine do insomniacs read in bed?
Snooze-week.

What did one doorbell say to another?
Have a wonderful chime.

What is a taxi's favorite vegetable?
Cab-bage.

How does a tailor answer people?
With fitting remarks.

Did you know there's a fiddle at the door?
Let the viol-in.

How did the nearsighted professor bump his head in the forest?
He didn't cedar tree.

Why are you writing on your sneakers?
I'm making a footnote.

Who cut the cannibal's hair?
A barber-ian.

What are a prisoner's favorite books?

Escape literature.

What is a moocher's favorite dessert?

Sponge cake.

Do you have your chicken delivered?

No, I just pullet along.

Can you answer the phone?

I can, but I don't know what the question is yet.

Hey, that sounds pretty good. What are you playing?

The piano.

What kind of conversation do people have on Thanksgiving?

They talk turkey.

I play the violin and tell jokes at the same time.
How can you tell what the people are laughing at?

Why don't you like my violin?
I do. I just don't like the sound it makes.

Are army cars expensive?
No, they're very Jeep.

Where does the mattress go every March?
Spring training.

Who started the lost and found?
Our Founding Fathers.

How does a 100-pound man sleep?
Lightly.

How did the prisoner escape from jail?

His face broke out.

If you give me $50, I'll get you a permanent job.

What is that?

Trying to get back the money.

Did you know you've been fired from every job you've ever had?

Well, nobody can call me a quitter.

Did you hear about the fire in the forest?

Yes, it was a tree-for-all.

Did the man who was arrested have a record?

No, but he's working on a CD.

What does a stonemason dance to?

Rock music.

I bought a cable-knit sweater.

What channels do you get on it?

Are you here again? Aren't you ashamed to be here?

What's good enough for you, Your Honor, is good enough for me.

What happened to the rustler who got a suspended sentence?

They hung him.

What country is noted for its autos?

Car-gentina.

Where do people who always alibi end up?

In the Hall of Blame.

What's a father's favorite health food?

Poppy seeds.

Where does the woman who colors her hair go for vacation?

To the bleach.

Why did the judge give the watch 30 days?

Because it wouldn't tock.

What would George Washington be if he were living today?

Over 250 years old.

Sixty days or a $6,000 fine. Which will it be?

The $6,000 would be fine, Your Honor.

What is the best tool to use when building a playground?
A see-saw.

Why did the Siamese twins get a traffic ticket?
For double parking.

Why should I keep my chin up?
It stops you from drooling on it.

Did you pick your nose?
No, I was born with it.

What is a Boy Scout's favorite dessert?
Cub cakes.

Why did Adam wear a fig leaf?
Because he didn't have any dates.

Why don't you take your brother Hans out to eat?

Because it's bad manners to eat with your Hans.

How does an angel answer the phone?

Halo.

I fell down yesterday.

Did you have a nice trip?

5. DOUBLE CROSSERS

Why didn't the nun ever change her clothes?
It was a bad habit.

Why did the ruler lose his job?
He didn't measure up to expectations.

How do you make a bandstand?
Play the Star Spangled Banner.

Why does the yeast go to bed at eight o'clock?
It's an early riser.

Why did you take the clock to the psychiatrist?
It was a cuckoo clock.

Why did the cannibal only eat thin people?
He was on a low-fat diet.

What do you get if you cross a five-dollar bill with a leopard?
Spot cash.

What do you get if you cross a bee with a rabbit?
A honey bunny.

What do you get if you cross a jackass with a comedian?
A man who laughs at his own jokes.

What do you get if you cross a tailor with Santa?
A person who hems and Claus.

What do you get if you cross a pickle with a flute?
Sour notes.

What do you get if you cross a police officer and a lens maker?
A captician.

What do you get if you cross a sofa and a kangaroo?
A couch with a pouch.

What do you get if you cross a cow and a weeping willow?
Someone who cries over spilt milk.

What do you get if you cross a telephone and Tarzan?

Ring Kong.

What do you get if you cross a watch with a bedbug?

A clock-roach.

What do you get if you cross an auto beeper with a box of cereal?

Horn flakes.

What do you get if you cross a magician with a clock?

A trick tock.

What do you get if you cross a policeman with a spider?

A cop-web.

What do you get if you cross a bakery item with a doorknob?

Bagels and locks (lox).

What do you get if you cross a lottery winner with a bank employee?

A fortune-teller.

What do you get if you cross an airplane with a baseball pitcher?

A flying tosser.

What do you get if you cross a rooster with yeast?

An early riser.

What do you get if you cross a skunk with a hornet?

A smelling bee.

What do you get if you cross a windowpane with a rabbit?

A glass hopper.

What do you get if you cross an airplane with a nagging spouse?

A flying bosser.

What do you get if you cross a policeman with a kitten?

A cop-y cat.

What do you get if you cross an elephant with a construction worker?

A very big dig.

What do you get if you cross bread with a famous children's story?

Pita Pan.

What do you get if you cross a small ship and a fantastic book?

A ferry tale.

What do you get if you cross a male parent and a watch?

Father Time.

What do you get if you cross a rubber band with a hired car?

A stretch limousine.

What do you get if you cross an ant with a leopard?

A good spot for a picnic.

What do you get if you cross a skeleton with a sheriff on horseback?

The Bone Ranger.

What do you get if you cross a policeman with a crybaby?

Cops and sobbers.

What do you get if you cross a famous spy with a magician?

James Wand.

Why is the magician walking with a cane?

He has a trick knee.

Why are you jumping up and down?

I just drank some spring water.

Was the watch mad when it was insulted?

Yes, it was ticked off.

What do two math teachers do with their lunch?

They divide it.

Is the doctor treating you?

No, I have to pay my own way.

Were the pills the trombonist took any good?

No, they had slide effects.

What is a bath's favorite line from Shakespeare?

Tub be or not tub be.

Why was the dermatologist unpopular?

He got under his patients' skin.

What pills work on you immediately?
Fast-pirin.

What happened to the Texan who struck oil?
He broke his wrist.

How does a baby doctor get paid?
Cash on delivery.

What does a dentist do while filling a tooth?
Fills his wallet.

6. BUT YOU LOOK GOOD

What could happen if I get a frog in my throat?
You might croak.

Did you ever get athlete's foot?
Yes. Joe kicked me so hard I could hardly sit down.

Two patients came into the doctor's office at the same time, one with a sore knee and the other with a sore throat. Who saw the doctor first?
The doctor put the cartilage before the hoarse.

What is that strange feeling I have in my head?
You have that empty feeling.

Is your cut very bad?
No. It stopped bleeding in the nick of time.

Did you have your teeth checked?
No. I don't think anyone will steal them.

What did one psychiatrist say to another?
You're feeling fine. How do I feel?

What's the best thing to do for lockjaw?
Get a locksmith.

What did you find out when you looked the gift horse in the mouth?
That it had bad breath.

Why did the pea go to the psychiatrist?
It had a split personality.

What kind of paper does a dermatologist write on?
A scratch pad.

Did you have anything to declare at the airport?
A nervous stomach.

When do doctors operate on royalty?
In the middle of the knight.

Why are you feeding your computer vitamins?
I don't want it to get a virus.

Why is a dentist like an army sergeant?
Both are drill masters.

My credit card expired.
I didn't know it was sick.

What's your hurry?
I've got insomnia and I'm going home to sleep it off.

Why are you riding up and down in the elevator?
The doctor told me to keep my foot elevated.

PATIENT: My husband thinks he's a car.
DOCTOR: Where is he now?
PATIENT: He's downstairs, double-parked.

DOCTOR: What can I do for you?
PATIENT: It's hard for me to make friends, you big, fat slob.

PATIENT: Why am I always worrying about money?
DOCTOR: Don't worry. I'll relieve you of that.

Why did the trumpet player go to the dentist?
For a toot canal.

Which tree is ailing?
The sycamore.

How did you break your wrist?
I punched the time clock.

Why did you wait 15 years to see a doctor when you swallowed a gold ring?
I was waiting till the price was right.

What's the best way to beat the flu?
With a strap.

What does the veterinarian wear when he examines a goat?
Kid gloves.

DOCTOR: Take the red pill first and then the white one.
PATIENT: What's the white one for?
DOCTOR: In case the red one is poison.

Did you cut yourself?
No, a razor blade did it.

What do you call an office worker who's always ill?
A sick-retary.

Why did the dog see the psychiatrist?
He kept barking up the wrong tree.

Why did the fat man become a psychiatrist?
So he could shrink on the job.

Why is the Doctor Rat very popular?
He makes mouse calls.

Why did the phone go to the doctor?
It had busy spells.

What is a dentist's favorite body of water?
The Root Canal.

You say the pill almost killed you?
Yes, it was supposed to make me look 10 years younger and I was eight at the time.

Are the teeth your own?
Yes, I just finished making the last installment.

Did you know he had false teeth?
Not until they came out in conversation.

Do your new pills have any side effects?
Yes, they make me poorer.

Why don't you put ice on your head for your headache?

It's no use, the cube keeps falling off.

Did you know that George Washington had wooden teeth?

Yes, he'd see his carpenter every six months.

How did you become an engineer when you were three years old?

I lied about my age.

How much do you charge to dig up data and trace back family lines?

$200 to have it dug up, and $600 to have it hushed up.

What does a cemetery worker sweep with?
A tomb-stick.

What happens when the gangster changes his address?
He makes false moves.

How does the magician answer the telephone?
Hello. Let me guess who this is.

7. DAFFYNITIONS

What do you call a person who steals boats?
A ship-lifter.

What is an optimist's favorite cowboy?
Hope-along Cassidy.

Who looks good at a beauty pageant?
The judges.

What is a shoplifter noted for?
The gift of grab.

What did one piccolo say to another?
Marry me and be my fife.

What's the best day for people who don't tell the truth?
Lie-day.

What's the best day to talk?
Chatter-day.

What is a duelist's favorite day?
Fence-day.

What is a priest's favorite baseball team?
The Saint Louis Cardinals.

What do you call a short-order cook who goes from job to job?
A fry-by-night.

What kind of house does the plumber have?
A wrench house.

How did the judge find his blanket?
Quilty.

What do you call a man in Nome who gets sunburned?
A baked Alaskan.

When is hot soup not hot soup?
When it's chili.

What is a snake's favorite vegetable?
An asp-aragus.

What's the best day to hang out clothes?

Dry-day.

What's the best day for a Peeping Tom?

Pry-day.

What do you call a tree that frequently calls pagers?

A beep-ing willow.

What do you call a person who's always criticizing an outdoor party?

A nit-picnicker.

Where do newspaper reporters eat?

In a press-taurant.

What is a fruit's favorite month?

Grape-ril.

What do you call a tailor who thumbs a ride?

A stitch-hiker.

What is a mean woman's favorite day?

Shrews-day.

Was the plane safe?

The safest on earth.

Why did the hen cross the road?

The chicken was on vacation.

How does a sheep rancher take care of his workers?

Shear and shear alike.

What is a fisherman's motto?

Stop, hook, and listen.

What kind of bathing suit does a wasp wear?

A bee-kini.

What did the silly boy do for the bang in his car?

He went to a dent-ist.

What kind of singers do you find among college faculty?

Tenures.

What is a detective's favorite vegetable?

Clue-cumbers.

What do you call a well-dressed fish?

A dapper snapper.

What does a detective use to clean his teeth?

Sleuth-paste.

What do you call a very dark café?
A guess-taurant.

Are gangsters rich?
Sure, they make a killing.

What does a priest have at the top of the room in his house?
Cathedral ceilings.

What do you call a handkerchief that's in a bad mood?
A cranky hanky.

8. GROANERS

Why is a the clock running?
It's trying out a new pair of sneakers.

What did the chicken say to the skeleton?
I've got a bone to pick with you.

What does Kris Kringle use when he burns himself?
Santa gauze.

What is a French bakery's favorite song?
Quiche me again.

What does the mollusk use to wash its hair?
Clam-poo.

What happens when you sit on a tack?
You get the point.

How did the judge punish the rubber band?
He sent him away for a long stretch.

What's a letter carrier's favorite magazine?
The Saturday Evening Postage.

How did the inchworm go crazy?
Trying to convert to the metric system.

How do you make an inkwell?
Send it to a doctor.

Did you take out the garbage?
It didn't want to go out with me.

What do you call a cat with a lot of nerve?
A pushy cat.

What is a watch's favorite candy?
Clock-olate.

What do you call a musical instrument that costs $1000?
A grand piano.

What's a computer's favorite ice cream?
Chocolate chip.

How would a barber answer if you got him angry?
With snippy remarks.

What did the minister say when he burned himself?
Holy smoke!

Why did the policeman arrest your belt?
Because it held up my pants.

What game did Dr. Jekyll like to play?
Hyde and seek.

Where do old candles wind up?
In a wax museum.

Why does your mother wear a hearing aid to bed?
My father talks in his sleep and my mother doesn't want to miss anything.

What insect gives all his friends gifts every Christmas?
Anty-Claus.

What do hairless people write with?
Bald-point pens.

Did you ever see a waterfall?
No, but I've seen a chocolate drop.

How is the sick computer feeling?
Chip-per.

How is your father's watch factory?
Not good. His business is winding down.

Does a rubber band ever lie?
No, but it stretches the truth a little.

How did the postmaster keep warm when the heat went out?
He stamped his feet.

How did the orange crash the party?
It squeezed in.

Are you wearing new shoes?
Yes, but I'm still wearing last year's feet.

Why are barbers usually undecided?
The don't know if they're going or combing.

What does a computer use to get in the house?
A keyboard.

How much are two and two?
I don't know. My computer's broken.

Did you ever listen to an elastic band?
No, but I've heard an engagement ring.

What do you call a hot dog that speaks its mind?
A frank furter.

Where does a raisin get its information?
Through the grape-vine.

How did the hatchet hurt himself?
It was an axe-ident.

Where are you going on your airplane trip?
Up.

Have you changed much since you stopped smoking and drinking?
Yes, I'm richer.

Did the arsonist get caught for setting fires?
Yes, he finally met his match.

Why did you put soap in your soup?
I wanted something to wash it down with.

Is the locksmith a good baseball player?
Sure, he's the key man.

What do Eskimos use for money?
Cold cash.

What's the favorite song for a baker?
There's no business like dough business.

Why are wood carvers happy people?
They whittle while they work.

Where does the tall man drive his car?
On the highway.

What is a traffic cop's favorite sweater?
A pullover.

What did the operator do when you put a slug in the pay phone?

She gave me the wrong number.

How does an undertaker know his business?

From the ground down.

Why do you go to bed with your insurance policy?

Because it covers everything.

What do you call an underwater swimmer in Havana?

A Cuba diver.

Why are you carrying a gun?

Because it's tired.

What do you get by gardening?

Bushed.

What's a carpenter's favorite song?
Awl of me.

What exercises do jewelers do?
Gemnastics.

What kind of jokes does the king of the jungle tell?
One-lioners.

9. PRO AND CORN

Why was the lawyer angry?
He made a cross examination.

How do Eskimos sleep?
With their eyes closed.

Do you mind your own business?
No, I have somebody working for me.

What do you call a gathering of gangsters at a barbecue?
A crook-out.

What do you use to fix a broken tuba?

A tuba glue.

Why is drinking milk like exercise?

They both strengthen the calves.

How do you make a bookend?

Stop reading.

Do you eat green vegetables?

I don't know. I'm color blind.

How do you build a cabinet?

First you have to become President.

Do you have trouble falling asleep?

No, I strap myself to the bed.

What do you grow in your garden?

Tired.

How do in-line skaters cut their toenails?

With roller blades.

What did one cannibal say to the other as they ate the clown?

Gee, he tastes funny.

Where do army servicemen eat off the post?

In a mess-taurant.

How long do you sleep at night?

Six feet, four inches.

Where does a bride put her husband when he doesn't behave?

In the groom closet.

What is a fog's favorite greeting?
How do you dew?

What would happen if you dropped the Thanksgiving platter?
It would be the downfall of Turkey, the overflow of Greece, and the destruction of China.

Do you have any fans in your house?
No, everybody hates me.

What caused the accident?
Two cars were after the same pedestrian.

Do you have a family tree?
No. My father does all the gardening.

What did one blackboard say to another?
Better slate than never.

Will you be long?
I don't think so. I'll always be short.

What did one stone say to another?
Slow down or you'll end up in the rocks.

What happened to the man in the plane crash?
He got an airline fracture.

How did you cut your mouth?
Eating swordfish.

What is the cleanest pastry?
A cake of soap.

Why did the silly kid plant a lightbulb in his garden?
So he could have a power plant.

What kind of treatment does a sick watch get in the hospital?

Around-the-clock care.

How do you make a lunchbox?

Get it a pair of fighter's gloves.

What's the most fragile thing in the world?

The dawn—it's always breaking.

Do you believe we should have a standing army?

No. They should be allowed to sit down once in a while.

What do you call a small fish that's been operated on?

A scar-dine.

Why did the lobster become a policeman?
He believed in claw and order.

How does a prisoner in jail like his food cooked?
Stir fried.

How do you make a doorstop?
Punish it.

Is the rubber ball still working?
No, it was bounced.

Why did you get all D's on your report card?
I must have had a low-grade infection.

Did you take the sleeping pill?
No, I didn't want to disturb it.

What do you call the pig who wins the lottery?
Filthy rich.

What is a prisoner's favorite bread?
A parole.

What are the twins' favorite fruit?
Pears.

What did one dictionary say to the other?
I'd like a word with you.

What is the singing dog's favorite movie?
The Hound of Music.

Why was the shooting star arrested?
It didn't have a gun license.

Would you like to go to Heaven someday?
Only with a return ticket.

What do you call a poor Texan?
A millionaire.

Was the carpenter tired?
He was awl in.

How does a bullfighter enter a house?
By the toreo-door.

Can you keep a secret?
No, we have no room in our house.

What handicap did the cabbage get in the road race?
A head start.

Did the potato enjoy himself?
He had a smashing time.

What's the favorite game for fish?
Finder's Kippers.

What do you call a fish with a good figure?
A svelte smelt.

10. YOU DON'T SAY

How do you like your new necktie?
Knot too good.

Why did you call the locksmith for your piano?
Two keys got stuck.

Do you sleep on your stomach?
No, on a mattress.

Does the Man in the Moon eat a lot?
Not when he's full.

What entertainment did Noah have for his guests?
An Ark-estra.

What does a monster eat with?
A fork lift.

What is a plumber's favorite dance step?
The tap dance.

How did you buy the watch?
Time payments.

When does the moon beam?
When you give it a compliment.

What kind of food is eaten quietly?
Shush-kebob.

What do you call a religious tooth?
A holy molar.

How did the weeping willow win first prize at the garden show?
For crying out loud.

What kind of stories does the captain of a ship tell his kids?
Ferry tales.

How did Napoleon meet his Waterloo?
He was introduced.

Did you like the Knights of the Round Table?
Yes, and I especially liked Sir Lance–a lot.

Didn't you see the raindrops?
I wasn't paying attention.

Where do angry skiers go?
On cross-country trips.

What do you call a hog that has several wives?
A pig-amist.

Do you still run errands for your mother?
No, I walk.

What is a Peeping Tom?
An unidentified spying object.

How was the bad candle punished?
He got 40 wax.

Did you fix the broken mirror yet?
No, but I'll look into it.

What has six legs and crawls?
Three babies.

Was your doctor visit expensive?
No, it was fee nominal.

Did you know that my baby sister is only 14 months old and she's been walking for four months?
Boy, she must be tired.

What time does your watch say?
It doesn't. It has laryngitis.

What do you call being employed by the Internal Revenue Service?
Taxing work.

Why shouldn't you give a little girl spaghetti at midnight?

Because it's pasta bedtime.

Taxi, are you engaged?

No, divorced.

Where do you look for a lost minister?

The Bureau of Missing Parsons.

What do you call a person who takes orders for cakes?

A cookie bookie.

Why did you make an addition to your house?

Because I wanted room for improvement.

What did one ice cream cone say to another?

Do me a flavor.

Do you carry a grudge?
No, I'm not supposed to lift anything.

What did one brick say to another?
You were cement for me.

When a boat sinks, what happens to its computer?
It gets chip-wrecked.

What did one poppy seed say to another?
I'm on a roll.

Who does a witch call for snacks when in a motel?
Broom service.

How poor were you?
We were so poor, the pigeons used to feed us.

What did one shoe say to the other?
Your lace is familiar.

What did one ear say to the other?
Watch out what you say. There's a nosy guy between us.

What did one sardine say to another?
See you when you get out of the can.

What happened at the Boston Tea Party?
I don't know. I wasn't invited.

Why are you exercising before you go to court?
I want to be fit to be tried.

Why is owning a tennis court a good investment?
It gives you a net profit.

How absentminded is he?
He's so absentminded, he sent his wife to the bank and kissed his money goodbye.

How small is your town?
So small, the only illness they allowed was smallpox.

How small is your hometown?
So small, they didn't allow double talk.

How small is your hometown?
So small, the baseball field only had three bases.

How small is your hometown?
So small, the police dog was a Pekingese.

How small is your hometown?
So small, the people ate only shortening bread.

How poor were you?
We were so poor, my mother kept our family together with cellophane tape.

What's a hot dog's favorite monster?
Frank-enstein.

What do you call an athlete who is not a regular on his team?
A scrub-stitute.

11. IT MAKES A DIFFERENCE

How did the butter get lost?
It took the wrong churn.

Did you hear about the musical burglar?
Yes. He was always breaking into song.

Why does smoke come out your chimney?
Smoking isn't allowed in the house.

Did you know you're walking the wrong way?
This is the only way I know how to walk.

What do you call a knife that cuts four loaves of bread at the same time?
A four-loaf cleaver.

How do you make money fast?
Stop feeding it.

If your umbrella has holes, why did you take it?
I didn't think it would rain.

Why did the burglar lose his job?
The only thing he could break into was a sweat.

What do you think of your babysitter?
She's OK, but I can think of many other things we need more.

Why couldn't Jack Horner escape?
Because he was cornered.

Just how poor were you?
We were so poor, we had to buy stamps on the installment plan.

Why didn't you steal second base at the game?
I couldn't. Too many people were watching me.

What tree is nosy?
A peeping willow.

How did you hear the phone from the bathroom?
By the ring around the tub.

Why don't grandfather clocks work much?
They're always striking.

How do you open a liquor store?

With a whis-key.

What kind of food did Romeo eat?

He ate what Juliet.

What's the difference between an enlightened person and a cruise ship at night?

One sees the light, the other lights the sea.

What's the difference between clouds and a tanning cream?

One hides the sun and the other suns the hide.

Why is a pig indoors like a house on fire?

The sooner both are put out, the better.

What's the difference between an escaped prisoner chased by policemen and a bug collector?

One flees cops and the other cops fleas.

Why is violin restoration like politics?

Both involve knowing how to pull strings.

What's the difference between a librarian and a theatrical agent?

One shows books and the other books shows.

What's the difference between a boxer who is knocked out and a self-centered duck?

One is down for the count and the other counts his down.

What's the difference between a plain-looking person and an animal hunter?

One prays for looks and the other looks for prey.

What's the difference between a plastic surgeon and a hitchhiker?

One lifts faces, the other faces lifts.

What's the difference between a bank teller and a lost motorist?

One signs checks, the other checks signs.

What's the difference between a caveman and a successful person?

One clubs heads and the other heads clubs.

What's the difference between a big spender and a podiatrist?

One foots the bill and the other bills the foot.

What's the difference between a music store and a car salesman?

One trades in drums and the others drums up trades.

What's the difference between a cop who arrests members of the judiciary and a book reviewer?

One books judges and the other judges books.

What's the difference between an angry ocean and a piece of male neckwear?

One is fit to be tide and the other is tied to be fit.

What's the difference between a person eating in the morning and a basketball team?

One breaks the fast and the other makes fast breaks.

What's the difference between a tourist and a travel agency?

One travels places and the other places travel.

What's the difference between a man counting money at a card game and a person reading in the dark?

One eyes his spoils and the other spoils his eyes.

What's the difference between a stationery clerk and a newspaper reporter?

One notes pens and the other pens notes.

What's the difference between a minister marrying a couple and a man putting on his neckwear?
One ties the knot and the other knots the tie.

What's the difference between a gangster and an arsenal?
One mans the guns and the other guns the man.

What's the difference between a bachelor and a baseball player?
One plays the field and the other fields the play.

What's the difference between a warranty and a guarantee?
The fine print.

What did the tree say when it was cut down?
Well, I'm stumped.

Did you hear anything about the fire in the barber shop?

Yes. It was a brush fire.

Why did you spit on that man?

His mustache was on fire.

What material are you using to build your puppy a home?

Dogwood.

How did the circus assistant die?

She was kissed by the sword swallower.

What did the football coach looking for a big lineman say when his wife gave birth to a 12-pound baby boy?

This is the end.

Index